D0669026

Sweeter Than Honey

Prayers for Catechists

ELIZABETH McMAHON JEEP

PRAY
today

ⱲⱢⱣ

WORLD LIBRARY PUBLICATIONS

The music and liturgy division of J. S. Paluch Company, Inc.

3708 River Road, Suite 400 • Franklin Park, Illinois 60131-2158

800 566-6150 • www.wlpmusic.com

Sweeter Than Honey

WLP 017351

ISBN 978-1-58459-572-4

Author: Elizabeth McMahon Jeep
Editor: Mary Beth Kunde-Anderson
Copy and Production Editor: Marcia T. Lucey
Typesetting and Design: Denise C. Durand
Director of Publications: Mary Beth Kunde-Anderson
Production Manager: Deb Johnston

Scripture excerpts from the *New American Bible with Revised New Testament and Psalms* © 1991, 1986, 1970, Confraternity of Christian Doctrine, Inc., Washington, DC. Used with permission. All rights reserved. No portion of the *New American Bible* may be reprinted without permission in writing from the copyright holder.

Scripture excerpt from *Lectionary for Mass for Use in Dioceses of the United States of America* copyright © 1998, 1997, 1970, Confraternity of Christian Doctrine, Inc., Washington, DC. Used by permission. All rights reserved. No part of the *Lectionary for Mass* may be reproduced by any means without permission in writing from the copyright owner.

English translation of the Antiphon from *The Liturgy of the Hours* © 1974, International Commission on English in the Liturgy Corporation. All rights reserved.

Excerpt from *A Book of Prayers* © 1982, International Commission on English in the Liturgy Corporation. All rights reserved.

Copyright © 2011, World Library Publications, the music and liturgy division of J. S. Paluch Company, Inc., 3708 River Road, Suite 400, Franklin Park, Illinois 60131-2158. All rights reserved under United States copyright law. No part of this work may be reproduced or transmitted in any form or format or by any means, whether mechanical, photographic, or electronic, including taping, recording, or photocopying, or any information storage and retrieval systems, without the express written permission of the appropriate copyright holder.

Table of Contents

How sweet to my tongue is your promise,
sweeter than honey to my mouth!

(Psalm 119:103)

Introduction: Using This Book

The first part of this book, "Praying with the Church," follows the liturgical seasons and draws its inspiration from the Sunday Gospels. Each reflection is named in a way that will help you find appropriate pages for meditation. The second section, "Praying with Students and Colleagues," includes blessings and meeting prayers that can be used alone, but most are meant to be prayed in a group. The last section, "Praying for the World," introduces themes not covered in the first or second section.

The book is intended for adult catechists and may be used alone, with a group of catechists, or with a group of adult students. Integrate it into your accustomed times of prayer, adapting the forms in a way that you find helpful. Most of the prayers begin with a short passage from the Bible followed by a reflection. You might sit in silence, light a candle, become calm and unhurried, read the words of the reflection thoughtfully, perhaps several times, pausing over phrases and ideas that catch your attention, and then move toward God who is present. Each reflection closes with the prayer itself—in italics—directed toward God. In the second and third sections, some prayers are set in roman typeface to facilitate their intended use as group prayer.

Entries can be expanded or reshaped for catechist meetings by adding introductory and closing dialogues (see "Dedication of the Year" for an example), passages from scripture, intercessions, rituals, or song.

It is hoped that regular use of the book will draw you gradually to penetrate more personally into the key mysteries of Christian faith, deepening your insight into the ministry of catechist, and enriching the more technical aspects of your teaching.

Praying with
the Church

Advent

Advent 1: Awake

It is the hour now for you to awake from sleep. For our salvation is nearer now than when we first believed; the night is advanced, the day is at hand.

Romans 13:11–12

wake up!
wake up! says the Church
consider Advent
the last chance
to prepare
for the Holy One
whom you have called upon
and seek unceasingly
yet whose coming
you have learned to dread
as a sign of judgment and loss
of time run out
for putting oil in lamps
or earning interest on unearned talents
a sign of the end of the world
as you know it

God of mercy
I do not fear your coming
for I am stumbling in the dark
and my world needs realignment
surely you will come again
as at the first
bringing order out of chaos
light to my soul
joy to my desperation
I will try to stay awake with Isaiah
practicing confidence
in a time of desperation
with Mary practicing patience
in a time of expectation
with my band of students
defying the darkness of the times
by building an evergreen wreath
and lighting its candles one by one
retelling the ancient stories
of promise and hope
singing again the prayer of longing
O come, O come, Emmanuel

Advent 2: Prepare

*On that day, a shoot shall sprout from the stump of Jesse
and from his roots a bud shall blossom.*

Isaiah 11:1

up now!
up now! says the Church
there's much to do before he comes
the sprout from Jesse's root about to bloom
drawing all nations to a new beginning
let us, then, make actual peace
in classroom, home, and public square
root out the lust for glory and power
that corrupts our people
the cosmic search for security
the wishful thinking
that blinds us to the dying going on
and leaves us stumbling in the dark
up now!
all is darkness
and there is much to do!

O patient God
what can my one small voice accomplish
perhaps it is enough
if I teach students
how to disarm the bully
protect the vulnerable
delight in giving
and helping
and listening
perhaps then we can make a difference
perhaps we few may be enough
to open up a place of welcome
for you, loving God
to come among our people
uniting us through your grace
grafting us onto Jesse's stump
where we can grow and flower
We look eagerly to that day, O Lord
and repeat our prayer of longing
O come, O come, Emmanuel

Advent 3: Rejoice

I rejoice heartily in the LORD
in my God is the joy of my soul.

Isaiah 61:10a

rejoice!
rejoice now! says the Church
even in the darkness
when the corrupt succeed
the devious break our hearts
the children march to wars no one can win
the planet melts
we suffocate on bills, plagues, pollution
and progress disguised as grace
commands allegiance
yes, even now, rejoice
for we have been commissioned
to bring glad tidings to the poor,
to heal the brokenhearted,
to proclaim liberty to captives
and release to prisoners
all fine reasons for rejoicing
if there were proof of such claims

I thank you God,
for letting us know what is coming
so that I can think it over in calm and stillness
as Mary did
pondering the part she would play
in your plan for the world
against all evidence
all common sense
I know that you are even now
moving more deeply into my domain
help me to do my part
to teach for peace as Isaiah did
to put things right as John directed
to bear the Light to all
who wait in darkness for your coming
as Mary did
confident that
Love is near
divine desire not human merit
the measure of your gift
as I wait
I sing with joy
O come, O come, Emmanuel

Advent 4: Emmanuel

*The virgin shall be with child, and bear a son, and shall name him
[E]mmanuel.*

Isaiah 7:14

a house is everything, said David
and he set about construction
of a temple
but no, said God
you are the only house I want
you, your children, your line
are home to me
a kingdom where my love can dwell
so God built from David's line
a holy temple, a kingdom home
that offered rest and grace
but it was incomplete
until in Mary's womb
another David grew
another home within the home that Mary knew
was built to house the One who loves
and saves our sorry lot

My God
I know that if I one day
like her
agree to house the living God
accept such grace
such mystery
such joy
accept the outrage of the Incarnation
then will my world turn upside down
and I will see fulfilled
everything that Advent promises
then will my presence
be grace to those I love
my words ring true with those I teach
and so with steadfast hope
I add my voice to the chorus
O come, O come, Emmanuel

Christmastime

Nativity of the Lord

The people who walked in darkness
have seen a great light;
upon those who dwelt in the land of gloom
a light has shone.

Isaiah 9:1

finally dawn breaks
the Light rising slowly
across the world
the Church bids us open our eyes
and with new vision
discover the very Word of God
source of all that has come to be
born into our history
revealed to us in mystery
wrapped in hidden majesty
this is a dawn like no other
for Light has come to gather us in
break our ties to darkness
open our eyes to the graced world around us
open our eyes to the intimacy with God
made possible at last

O God
keeper of promises
my heart echoes the joyful praise of angels
glory and welcome to you who love us
who have come to live and to grow among us
bringing peace and divine favor
I join shepherds hastening to see
for themselves the meaning of this good news
and with them offer the only adequate
the only possible response
joyful praise and grateful adoration
Gloria in excelsis Deo

Christmastime

The Holy Family

He went down with them and came to Nazareth, and was obedient to them; and his mother kept all these things in her heart. And Jesus advanced [in] wisdom and age and favor before God and man.

Luke 2:51–52

not the household you planned, Joseph?
(pregnant bride, mysterious child)
do not be afraid to outgrow dreams
("Joseph and Sons" above the shop
self-replication, honor in the town)
like father Abraham do not be afraid
to open your door to strangers
and discover God among the guests
a better plan at work
than any you could design
(the bearer of good news
standing by your side,
the very hand of God placed in your own)
live the mystery within the mystery
of family life

motherhood not what you had expected, Mary?
divine child nestled in your embrace
your eyes feasting
on the One you have awaited in faith
but as you spend each lovely day together
you know as every mother does
that childhood is over in a flash
home base temporary
teach him of his people's history and hopes
the chanting of their psalms
the import of their prayers

and so prepare him
and you
for the day of his leaving

Gracious God
awaken me
during this Christmas season
to see in every home
a harbor for the Christ
shelter where truest Love can grow
where each
in the other's eyes
can see Emmanuel
I ask this in the name of Jesus
newborn among us
Amen

Christmastime

Epiphany

Where is the newborn king of the Jews? We saw his star at its rising and have come to pay him homage.

Matthew 2:2

is it wise, do you think
to pack up in the middle of winter
and ride off in search of an infant king
by following a star
an untrustworthy lot, the stars
likely to flicker and die
leaving a person stranded and foolish
luring the unwary to God-knows-what
maybe nothing
or everything
does wisdom lie in staying home
or risking safety, name, and treasure
to seek a mystery

you must choose
wisely

in the business of stars
no certainty but this:
whether you go
or stay
you will be changed forever

Loving God
each day's journey
brings me closer to you
teach me to be a wise traveler
let your word guide me
as a star guided the wise ones of old
and keep me alert for signs of your dwelling
welcome me when I arrive
and receive with joy the gifts I bring:
my praise and gratitude
my love
my care for others

bless the students who think me wise
and look to me for guidance
keep me an honest teacher
pointing to your wisdom
as the only guiding star
I ask this in the name of
Jesus our Emmanuel
Amen

Christmastime

Flight into Egypt

Joseph rose and took the child and his mother by night and departed for Egypt. He stayed there until the death of Herod.

Matthew 2:14–15a

Sometimes you just have to move on, Joseph,
leave the life
you worked so hard to build
the client list
the easy chair
the Sabbath routines
that give a man shape in his community
today the dream changes
the Lord asks more:
join immigrants on their dangerous road
take only essentials
urgency overcoming inconvenience
retrace the path your namesake
followed centuries ago
seek safety for your wife and child
among a people
who have not forgotten how to dream

merciful God

you have called me to be a teacher
bearing Christ safely to a new generation
you alone command my destiny
you alone my goal, my path, my guide
be light to my journey
for I cannot see beyond the next turning
strengthen my courage and give me peace
in the name of Jesus your Son
Amen

Christmastime

Baptism of the Lord

After Jesus was baptized, he came up from the water and behold,
the heavens were opened for him, and he saw the Spirit of God
descending like a dove and coming upon him. And a voice came from
the heavens, saying, "This is my beloved Son, with whom I am well
pleased."

Matthew 3:16–17

he burst from the water
as the sun at creation
full of promise and purpose
rose from the river's womb
washed and anointed
a newborn of dual heritage:
generous earth mother
well-pleased Father God
his person
an epiphany of incarnate purpose
ultimate reconciliation
of flesh and spirit
divine adoption
human transcendence

Spirit-impelled
he enters the splintered world
as light to the nations
sight to the blind
justice to the oppressed
healing to the desperate
peace to the divided
consolation to the destitute
good news
in a wintry season

God of creation
renew in me baptismal clarity
purpose
and confidence
send me as you sent your Son
to be good news to family, students, parish
let me bring peace and wisdom
healing and hope
to all those who seek the God of Israel
Amen

Ordinary Time: Winter

Candlemas

[A] light for revelation to the Gentiles,
and glory for your people Israel.

Luke 2:32

God of winter
your light is slow in coming
and we wait with impatience
in the chilly darkness
of this winter world

how is it that Simeon recognized you
in the average-looking newborn
how did he discern your light
in the darkness of political corruption
Roman occupation
a demoralized people

how did Anna know
the prayerful widow
who gave thanks
and spoke about the child
to those who would listen
those who had been waiting in expectation
were there many
who trusted the word of these holy prophets
seeing in the eyes of Anna and Simeon
light and warmth they could not discern on their own
did they treasure the wisdom of their elders
in a way our people have forgotten

God of winter
put a light in my eyes
and a lightness in my spirit
that I may turn from all that is dark
and limited and negative
and discern your hidden presence
in the shining eyes of those around me
let your light and warmth
shine through my words
so that students may recognize
and give thanks
that you are here
though hidden, as always
among the seemingly average and unremarkable
among those who have been waiting in expectation
Amen

Ordinary Time: Winter

Called

When they brought their boats to the shore, they left everything and followed him.

Luke 5:11

it must have caused some whispering
over the fences in Capernaum
four fine fishermen
hard workers, good providers
leaving father, boats, nets, wives perhaps, and
children
leaving everything
for what
membership in a band of the born-again
evangelists of a new dispensation
why not compromise:
preach locally
and maintain the fishery
true religion shouldn't be so costly
or were they glad to leave it all behind
the daily struggle with the sea, torn nets
wholesale brokers from the city
why not follow a dream almost forgotten
since their youth
of giving themselves to the community
in a way that would matter
the preacher from Nazareth
just might be the One they had waited for
since the time of David
it was the opportunity of a lifetime
they decided
and so, gladly, left their fear
along with their boats
and followed

Jesus of Nazareth,
grant me a fisherman's decisiveness
I too have heard your invitation
and have joined your company
freely and gladly
but now I am exhausted
from trying to drag my boat along behind
in case I need some of my "stuff"
later
Holy One of God,
teach me to recognize my fear
of lightening my load
teach me to observe in my students the joyful freedom
of uncomplicated self-giving
Amen

Ordinary Time: Winter

The Beatitudes

Blessed are the poor in spirit,
for theirs is the kingdom of heaven.

Matthew 5:3

though framed as a single sermon
it is a compendium of teachings
meant to comfort members
of a persecuted church
a teaching too dense, too deep
to be fully understood
by a bystander
it is a teaching meant to prepare for the time
when Christian character is put to the ultimate test

we are mourning today as in ages past
for, in Africa and the Middle East,
in China and the Pacific
Christians are denied their rights, tortured,
burned out of homes and churches, murdered
and yet remain clean of heart, poor in spirit
showing mercy and not retaliation
seeking lasting peace not just for themselves
but for all who suffer injustice
they are indeed "children of God"
receiving comfort and divine mercy
supporting one another,
making Christ visible in their person
and in their communities of love

God of endless mercy
let your teaching take root in me
so that it can be understood by my students
not as a lesson to be learned
but a life to be lived
let me be a teacher in your image
speaking the truth with conviction
and acting with compassion, mercy, and peace
protect and support all those who suffer unjustly
for their religion or other minority condition
and be present to my students
with the grace of your Spirit
when they are put to the test
Amen

Ordinary Time: Winter

Vine and Branches

Just as a branch cannot bear fruit on its own unless it remains on the vine, so neither can you unless you remain in me. I am the vine, you are the branches.

John 15:4–5

it is a nice image
but a hard teaching
we are living branches
bound to Christ
entwined with one another
in a living unity
rooted in his love
his grace
his mission
we cannot break away
and still live
but we who worship independence
prefer to set a limit to belonging
keep religion personal
which is to say self-chosen
upbeat
find a liturgy we can relate to
a parish with our kind of people
ministry without meetings
no meddling in politics
no face-to-face with the poor
everything cool and reasonable
but surely that can't be enough
it doesn't feel like life
coursing through a growing
vibrant, fruitful vine

God of compassion
you ask that I love you
and all those others you bring into my life
but that is more than I can give
I am afraid of losing myself
of being swallowed up
in other people's lives
I cannot do it
unless it is your own love
passing through me
to others
and through others to me
Christ the Vine
keep me rooted firmly in the soil
of your grace
and in the unity of your Church
Amen

Ordinary Time: Winter

Carnival

I give you thanks that I am fearfully, wonderfully made;
wonderful are your works.

Psalm 139:14

how seldom do we celebrate the physical
fully, ungrudgingly, religiously
grant ourselves permission
to indulge in the purely pleasurable
the Irish enjoy a well-watered wake
Mexicans remember their dead
at midnight in a marigold-bedecked cemetery
Americans hide their ritual of giving and receiving
under miles of Christmas ribbon
but for the most part
Christians are a pretty tame lot
saving our sacraments for church
and letting Pilgrim ancestry
win out over our pagan DNA
yet Christians still can see the face of God
behind the masks of earth-bound revelry
and so keep Carnival as a holy season
a time to uncork our passions,
delight in the strength of human desire,
fortify ourselves against the heresy
that Lent is the only place where Christians
feel at home

God our Creator
you have made us with utmost skill
and called us and all creation good
I give you thanks
and honor my body
and its various enjoyments
however earthy and robust:
the taste of mouth-watering food, heady drink
the poetry of lace and silk
the exuberance of stand-up comedy
snowball fights and bug collecting
and sex of course—paradigm of sacred covenant

in due time I shall enter Lent with its sobering balance
but for now I will celebrate Carnival
eating pancakes and paczki
hanging gaudy decorations
singing vigorous songs of gratitude
and I shall rejoice
that the entirety of life is sacrament
Amen

Lent

Ash Wednesday

Behold, now is a very acceptable time; behold, now is the day of salvation.

2 Corinthians 6:2

now! says the Church
Lent is here
do you have time for it
time to get it organized
time to make a good plan
daily Mass perhaps
some fasting
hidden deeds of mercy and love
Lord knows,
those who need mercy are not lacking
but so little time
it will be gone before you know it

now! says the Church
here is a singular opportunity
enough time
as teacher, as family, as Christian
to make good plans
to simplify
to reflect, rededicate
to return to your God
with ashes
and enthusiasm

come, Lord Jesus,
open my mind to the possibilities of this holy season
let me embrace voluntary restraint,
practice the kind of self-forgetfulness
that creates community,
help me to take prayer seriously,
give generously to the poor,
and to fast in such a way that I become
uncomfortable with the comfort in which I live
teach me patience as I dwell in the desert with you
for forty days and forty nights
and let my conversion be a recommitment
to the loving relationships
with which you have blessed my life
Amen

Lent

Lent 1: Temptation

Jesus was led by the Spirit into the desert to be tempted by the devil.
He fasted for forty days and forty nights, and afterwards he was hungry.

Matthew 4:1

Spirit-led into the desert
we have made of once-lush Eden
we are given forty days
to ask hard questions

why should we not turn stones to bread
satisfy our every hunger
stash all that we can gather
be comfortable
where's the harm in living well

why should we not seek power
build a kingdom through forthright self-assertion
the other way
binding ourselves in love and trust
is slow and tedious
regrettably unreliable
let's use the tools that win the game

why should we not challenge God
demand salvation, safety for the risks we take
why not rely on angels, awe, and arrogance
dazzle with lofty gesture
now there's a religion people will respect
desert clarity, cool gospel light
won't sell

God of the desert
help me during this precious forty days
to spot temptation in the clutter of my noisy life
to sort reality from counterfeit
to explore again my heart and head
to feel an honest hunger
I ask your strength
your presence
your guidance
Amen

Lent 2: Transfiguration

Then Peter said to Jesus in reply, "Rabbi, it is good that we are here! Let us make three tents: one for you, one for Moses, and one for Elijah."

Mark 9:5

we know what transfiguration means
because we too have struggled up the mountain
following Jesus
to the very top
where we were blinded
by the vision
of his dazzling reality
embodiment of a new covenant,
revelation of God's glory
thus we work hard at being catechists
preparing lessons
mixing paints
praying over each student's needs
in order to share the vision
awaken in others the certainty
of mystery
we teach because we must
because we have seen Jesus
easy to say
impossible to explain
important to treasure

Christ of the mountaintop
like other disciples
I have experienced your mystery
yet feel the instinct to build shrines
to house you
so that in times of stress and doubt
I can revisit the experience
and again be filled with conviction
send your Spirit to transfigure me
from believer of truths
to visionary
Amen

Lent 3: Living Water

If you knew the gift of God . . . you would have asked him and he would have given you living water.

John 4:10a, b

not half of forty days is gone
yet patience strains
and desert thirst is sharp
we long for living water
and come with empty buckets to the well

we try to grasp the word he tells us there
about worshiping in spirit and truth
testing traditions for authenticity
replacing false lovers with genuine God
but it does not follow customary logic
our proper way of knowing things
and we are left unsettled
we see that he sees
through our disguises
shows us our truer selves
well-loved
the object of his search
our meeting, then
is no chance encounter
he has tracked us down
in the city, the grocery
the kitchen, bedroom, schoolyard
and speaks to each of us
and to all of us together
so that we no longer
believe on the word of others
but know for ourselves
that he is water for a thirsty world

God of Jacob's well
refresh me with your truth
about myself
my loves, my practices
purify my faith and my desire
give me water
in the desert
Amen

Lent 4: Light of the World

*Night is coming when no one can work. While I am in the world,
I am the light of the world.*

John 9:4b–5

does he mean that we are blind
do not see him clearly
don't see much of anything clearly
spend our lives stumbling about in the dark
and wearing mismatched socks
then enough of blindness
turn on the light
pull up the shades
open our eyes

but light is painful to the unaccustomed eye
conversion upsetting
do we pray
God give us vision
but not too much
we have apple carts to keep upright
Pharisees to impress
neighbors to think about
we will have to meet them differently
if we see them differently
if we become a people of vision
if seeing one another
we see you
God give us vision
is a dangerous prayer

Christ of Siloam
the healing pool
cure my limited vision
open my eyes to the needs of my family
my students, colleagues, friends
open my eyes to the world of suffering
hidden behind each headline
each story of disaster and disease
open my eyes
and send me to the despised, the depressed
the dispossessed
give me strength to be your light to them
give me strength to pray
God give me vision
Amen

Lent 5: Resurrection and Life

I am the resurrection and the life; whoever believes in me, even if he dies, will live, and everyone who lives and believes in me will never die.

John 11:25–26

the one he loves is dead
and he is weeping
O my people, he says
I would open your graves
and have you rise
I am your resurrection
I am your life

so many of our family are dying
brothers and sisters
tied hand and foot with burial bands
the body of Christ
itching for resurrection
and Jesus himself deeply troubled
take away the stone, he commands
untie them and let them go

where are those who see clearly
and trust absolutely
who will tell him
that we are dead
and urge him to come with haste

Jesus of Bethany
prophet of life
free me of all that binds me to death
that my hands may lift up my students
that my feet may take me to your side
wherever I see you suffering and bound
I weep with you over all the lost
the isolated, the imprisoned
put your words of hope and love
in my mouth
that I too may bring life and freedom
to your people
Amen

Lent

Palm Sunday
of the Passion of the Lord

Kneeling, he prayed, saying, "Father, if you are willing, take this cup away from me; still not my will but yours be done."

we hold the branches and recall
the youthful, palmy days of our discipleship
when life was all hosannas
then comes the Passion story
to remind us how it all worked out
here is the extravagant woman, the traitorous friend
the dinner of sacrifice that no one understood
fearful struggle in the garden
(proof, if there was any doubt, of his humanity)
blustery Peter frightened by an honest question
his faith (not in Jesus but in himself) undone
and Pilate, high priest, Sanhedrin
pasting up a case
bending laws to meet political needs
finally out it comes: are you the Christ?
the answer swift and to the point: I am!
and the game is up—the future sealed
inevitably the cry for crucifixion
give us Barabbas, we can handle him
we understand him
but this one is a mystery
lead him away

so it is done
and all the earth is stilled
suspended
waiting

Jesus of Gethsemane
I wait with all Jerusalem
I know the outcome of this story
but do not look ahead
stay with the death a while to feel its sting
to probe the mystery of love
the passion hidden in your Passion
that proves me loved and chosen
and promises something more to come
Jesus, savior
let me walk through the coming days with you
and with your Church
let me live your mystery
that I may one day share in your glory
Amen

Triduum and Eastertime

Thursday of the Lord's Supper

He poured water into a basin and began to wash the disciples' feet.
"As I have done for you, you should also do."

John 13:5, 15

the disciples were assembled
the room prepared,
the feast of Passover freedom about to begin
when there was a small deviation from tradition

servant-like, he washed their feet
and urged them to similar works of service
a short but essential
education in humility
then came the prayers, the meal
and the second
greater interruption:
this is my body broken for you
this cup is the new covenant in my blood
only later did they understand
that this meal was the turning point
in his ministry
in their call
to liberate a new generation
through water and spirit
through leadership in service
through the sharing of bread and cup
thus would his presence
continue
to shape their lives
and the life of their community
in freedom and love
through all of time

God of unfailing love
you have called me
through the rebirth of baptism
to vigorous life in the sacramental community
cleanse the Church itself
through the celebrations of these holy days
that your message and your grace
may be renewed in us
so that all of us may
recognize and root out
everything that is unworthy
of your holy people
I pray this through Christ, our Lord
Amen

Triduum and Eastertime

Friday of the Passion of the Lord

Then he said to them, "My soul is sorrowful even to death. Remain here and keep watch." When he returned he found them asleep. . . . And they all left him and fled.

Mark 14:34, 37, 50

In a time of dread and agony
he was left alone
that is the saddest part
we sleep through the suffering of others
send our children off to war
hoping they won't come back damaged
brush past outstretched hands of the homeless
write "get well" cards to the dying
watch the TV news trying to remember
if all those victims were on our side or not
a better question:
are we are on God's side or not
for Christ is there
suffering and dying

while we can barely stay awake

I have known Good Friday
I have seen the good die young
with so much promise
gone in an instant
or in a long slow dying
I have seen good people crushed
isolated, ridiculed, silenced, closeted
even among my students
I have seen the scars
I have carried burdens too heavy to manage
doomed to failure
had painstaking work undone
by wrongheaded people in power
I have known darkness that no words could lighten
when someone stood with me
quietly, with no demands
and it was saving grace to me
so I will wait with you, my Christ
today
and whenever I find you suffering
Amen

Easter Sunday
of the Resurrection of the Lord

Why do you seek the living one among the dead? He is not here, but he has been raised.

Luke 24:5–6

awake, and hear the women singing
come, witness the impossible
the giant stone, our primal fear
rolled back
the dead, the lonely, the failed, the despairing
all are raised, renewed, begraced
for he is risen
how beautiful the day
how beautiful the body gathered here
called from the tomb of Lent
hungry from the fast
ready for the feast
let those who repented, sing
those who found new faith, rejoice
those who were forgiven, embrace
don flowered hats and dancing shoes
hold hands with neighbors
welcome outcasts to your table
crack Easter eggs in ceremony
for he is risen
alleluia
let the whole fragrant world
breathe alleluia

Risen Christ,
give me an Easter heart
and teach me to rejoice
I know an empty tomb
still leaves unanswered questions
faith stretched to the breaking point
yet I also know that you are here
offering me your peace
and joy
so I will join my community
in Easter faith
and Easter alleluias

Easter 2: Doubting Thomas

Blessed are those who have not seen and have believed.

John 20:29

don't stand there staring Thomas
come and touch me, says Jesus
have faith
become familiar with my damaged condition
you will recognize me
in villages and upper rooms
in rehab units, alleyways
schoolrooms, neighborhoods
and battlefields
touch me with healing power
you saw how it was done
when I touched the blind man
the dying girl
the boy who could not speak
it takes great faith Thomas
you are right to hesitate
perhaps you are the only one
who sees the consequence of faith
let it in and your separate life is over
you are one with me
you are my body
suffering, scarred, saved and saving
these are my Easter gifts to you, Thomas
abiding faith
unhesitating compassion
a healing touch

Jesus, Emmanuel
visit me in your risen body
as you came to Thomas
full of encouragement
and love
bring Easter gifts to me
for the sake of my students
abiding faith to guide my teaching
unhesitating compassion
especially for those who try my patience
and a healing touch for each one
who is struggling
to carry some burden I know nothing of
they have come to me
to find the Church
to find you
be with us as you have promised
Amen

Triduum and Eastertime

Easter 3: Emmaus

*The two recounted what had taken place on the way and how he was
made known to them in the breaking of the bread.*

Luke 24:35

we still take that road
for market days and festivals
and the way is mined with memories
of that time when
grieving and dismayed
we met a stranger
who brought light to our confusion
and tarried to break bread with us
I don't know why we were chosen
we weren't the brightest
or the most devoted followers
but there he was at our table
and we were his

since then we look closely at each stranger
smile at every passerby
because you never know
and often there are glimpses
of the one we seek
it makes for a slower journey
but when the day is overcast
our way a jumble
we see in those around our table
proof that our redeemer lives

Risen Jesus,
I too catch glimpses
of your face
in those around me
especially those who suffer without bitterness
who study the words of scripture
and live by its wisdom
who center their lives in the Eucharist
fill them with your grace
and Easter joy
Amen, Alleluia

Triduum and Eastertime

Easter 4: Good Shepherd

I am the good shepherd, and I know mine and mine know me.

John 10:14

a tribe of nomads
leading their flocks
from one watering hole to another
over the centuries
became convinced
that their paths were not random
but carefully planned
by One who had chosen them
guided them
watched with them through the night

strengthened by shepherd patriarchs
guided by shepherd leaders
championed by shepherd kings
they learned to address their Holy One
with all respect and tenderness
as the Shepherd of Israel
who knows, loves, protects his sheep
now the Son has come
to take his place beside the Father's flock
has laid down his life to protect them
has picked it up again
to lead them home

it is a clear theme
a single image
four thousand years and more in the making

just and loving God
why are so many of your sheep
wandering away
following other voices
into other pastures
I hear the howling of wolves
here within your sheepfold
I tire of putting a good face on things
that need changing
strain to remain loving
grace filled in the struggle
something is clearly wrong among your followers
perhaps we have too long
acted as if we were truly sheep
Good Shepherd
be with your Church as you have promised
speak to my students
they long to hear your voice
Amen

Triduum and Eastertime

Easter 5: The Way, the Truth, the Life

Where I am going you know the way.

John 14:4

the way is way too complicated
full of potholes, unexpected turns
and the truth is not at all as clear
as it was in our salad days
when the world seemed just a hair from saved
and we were winning all the arguments
and as for life
just look around
there is too much dying going on
we've tried to find the way
hear the truth
lay hold of life
during each commercial break
but we planted rules not roses
doctrines not daffodils
and none have flowered

you have it wrong, says Jesus
I AM the way, draw near
I AM the truth that matters
I AM the life you need
the joy, the hope
come and see
and sing out alleluia

Risen Jesus
give me the words to help my students
look for your living presence
their source and their stability
in the life of faith
show yourself to them
and to me
when we are confused about your teaching
or burdened with religion's
rites and claims and practices
remind me always that you alone
are guidance, wisdom, and life
for me
Amen

Easter 6: Love One Another

This is my commandment: love one another as I love you.

John 15:12

I am in the Father
and you are in me
and I am in you
and the Spirit makes us one
that is all I have come to teach
once you know it
I am fully revealed

I do not watch you
from a distance
parceling out grace
for commandments kept
you who are joined to me
keep my commandments
because you see them whole
as parts of a whole life
a whole heart
the expression of your very being
you in me
and I in you
such is the harmony of love

God of mercy
you promise that if I am truly loving
I will be filled with joy
so again it all comes down to love
wholehearted
steadfast
all-embracing love
when I would rather settle
for something less
tolerance of students who lose their books
patience with parents
who honor the student's hockey game
instead of Sunday Mass
condescension toward other catechists
who can't find the book of Exodus
perhaps my lack of joy
is a measure of my distance from the goal

love is your gift, my God
I stand with my arms outstretched
Amen

Triduum and Eastertime

Ascension of the Lord

The Lord Jesus, after he spoke to them, was taken up into heaven and took his seat at the right hand of God. But they went forth and preached everywhere.

Mark 16:19–20

we catechists sometimes get lost in trivia
rummage in our attic
for "fun facts" about religion
old saints and new devotions
trying to keep the doctrines straight
perfect in each detail
because we are not quite sure
which detail God finds essential

only this is essential:
the gospel in its simplicity
I am the message, says Jesus
I am the gift
of the Father's love
so be at peace
wait for the Spirit to give you courage
and help you sort it all out
I shall move ahead
into the whole world
where I shall wait for you
in my new body
don't just stand in awe
but go
be my witnesses
my body
my gospel

Divine Wisdom,
I try to keep my teaching authentic
clear and true
an expression of my faith
and of my studies
and my prayer
let the voice of your Spirit
enrich my teaching
enliven my community
inspire my Church
to become true witnesses
to the ends of the earth
Amen

Easter 7: The Word of the Lord

*Now they know that everything you gave me is from you, because the
words you gave to me I have given to them.*

John 17:7–8

knowing that his mission is drawing to a close
Jesus surveys the followers
gathered at his final feast
a diverse group
fishermen, tax collectors, scholars
poor and wealthy, men and women,
the cautious and the impetuous
and as on the sixth day of creation
he sees that it is good
he has given them his words
as he was sent to do
and though they still have much to learn
they have grasped the heart of it
they have trust in him
and in the One who sent him
they have the faith
and the will to follow him to the ends of the world
he offers one last prayer on their behalf
one last request:
that they may be one
as strongly bound as the Trinity itself
in love and truth

Father,
I make the prayer of Jesus my own
I pray for unity in the Church
especially among those
who have taken his words to heart
and who serve the Church as catechists
bless us with strong faith
the ability to grasp the meaning of your word
determination to teach with joy and delight
and hearts large enough to gather in all who come to us
make me worthy of my calling
and one with you
in Christ Jesus
Amen

Triduum and Eastertime

Pentecost

They were all filled with the Holy Spirit and began to speak in different tongues, as the Spirit enabled them to proclaim.

Acts 2:4

the Church is burning
with love or hatred who can say
the roaring wind uproots our very history
and we in panic rush to rescue this or that
not knowing artifact from essence
voices rise, struggling for attention
but who can find the meaning
who decode the proclamation
are these the signs that we were promised
divine breath, cleansing fire, unifying word,
or smoke and mirrors
mere semblance of the Spirit's visitation

do not be afraid
know that here in chaos
under signs of wind and fire
and language that is not culture-bound
the Spirit moves,
fair Wisdom opens ears, loosens tongues
untangles the syntax of competing claims
and misleading verities

be strong
know that the Spirit of God is with the Church
inspiring wise and courageous teachers
leaders filled with faith
prayerful members
intent on asking authentic questions
of a loving God

Come, Holy Spirit
fill my heart with your love
my mind with your teaching
my hands with the tools of my mission
Come, Spirit of the Church
guide and enlighten me
fill me with energy
to model what I teach
and inspire others
with your gift of amazing grace
Come, Spirit of Truth
Amen

Ordinary Time: Summer, Fall

The Most Holy Trinity

Go, therefore, and make disciples of all nations, baptizing them in the name of the Father, and of the Son, and of the Holy Spirit.

Matthew 28:19

"one God in three divine Persons"
so say creed and catechism,
but the words do not reveal
the reality we know
we hunger for more
for something that will explain what we know
to strangers
and to ourselves
we comb the sacred texts for definitions
to be memorized
and find only metaphors to be pondered
a gentle breeze passing by our cave
a powerful wind bringing life from primordial ooze
alpha and omega
mighty king, loving shepherd
rock, fortress
and suddenly it all adds up
to something
we are amazed to discern the mystery
of God in essence one, in presence three
of God in human flesh
of Body broken, risen, given
of many, one
against all logic
we can rejoice, and be at peace
and each in native tongue
and words of personal encounter
invite the listener's faith and praise

Divine Trinity
you claimed me in baptism
named me as your own
and signed me with the cross
through which your saving love
has conquered sin and death
in the company of all your chosen people
with care and gratitude
I confirm our bonds
in the name of the Father
and of the Son
and of the Holy Spirit
Amen

Ordinary Time: Summer, Fall

The Most Holy Body and Blood of Christ

Then he took the bread, said the blessing, broke it, and gave it to them, saying, "This is my body, which will be given for you; do this in memory of me." And likewise the cup after they had eaten, saying, "This cup is the new covenant in my blood, which will be shed for you."

Luke 22:19–20

the disciples were assembled
the room prepared, the meal ready
the Passover prayers
proclaimed their people's ancient flight from slavery
protected by the blood of the lamb
nourished by its flesh and with unleavened bread
and then
a postscript
this is my body broken for you
this cup is the new covenant in my blood
with those few words
Jesus became the sacrificial Lamb of a new people
source of their freedom
their membership in a new covenant
the mystery of God-with-us
took on a new dimension
defying time and space
a single and singular Real Presence
under the appearance of bread and wine
in the flesh and blood of his every follower
in the least particle of created matter in the universe

it is a personal yet universal call
repeated week by week, year by year
"The Body of Christ"
"The Blood of Christ"
to which we reply
"Amen"

Saving God,
I am learning to appreciate
week by week, year by year
the enormity of the grace put into my hands
how coherent, how clear, how expansive
is the body of Christ
how small, how self-serving,
how clumsy, even arrogant my normal vision of things
yet you continually invite me to the table
that through him
and with him
and in him
I too may extend that mystery in time and space
until he comes again
Amen

Ordinary Time: Summer, Fall
The Caring Community

They came bringing to him a paralytic carried by four men. Unable to get near Jesus because of the crowd, they opened up the roof above him. After they had broken through, they let down the mat on which the paralytic was lying. When Jesus saw their faith, he said to the paralytic, "Child, your sins are forgiven."

Mark 2:3–5

Mark draws a picture of the perfect Catholic parish
neighbors crowding into the house of Jesus
upon a Sabbath morning
intent upon his words
wondering at his signs
attentive, curious
knowing somehow that more is happening
than they can quite put their finger on
and suddenly four hearty believers
with missionary inspiration
(catechists perhaps, parents, caring friends)
scoop up one whose need is great
who wants to come, to join
but cannot make a move

finding the normal entry blocked
they blast through the roof
knowing that their job
is just to make the introductions
that Jesus can handle things from there

Jesus, our healer
many among us are paralyzed
unable to come to you without the support
of this community
bless those in my parish
who keep track of the isolated
the frightened
the hesitant learners
inspire me to become attentive to them
to encourage them
to awaken them
to become creative in bringing them
to you
that much I can do
the rest is up to you
Amen

Ordinary Time: Summer, Fall

John the Baptist

What did you go out to see? A prophet? Yes, I tell you, and more than a prophet.

Luke 7:26

John settled at the water's edge
close to the abyss
in which true life was to be found,
encouraged listeners to risk everything
and follow him into the river
repent, he said, wash away the falsehood
that eats into your very substance
purify your mind, your hope, the life you lead
plunge in and live

and many of the strong stepped into the river
felt the flood sweep away
failures, false starts, and outright sins
but also pleasures and plans, opinions, strategies,
treasured constructions of a lifetime
upended in a flash
glorious calamity
tsunami of the spirit
it left them reeling on the shore

repentance is a dangerous thing
it does not take half measures
nor dwell in yesterday like mere regret
but yields to deconstruction
sees with awe familiar mountains leveled
rocky paths made smooth
then struggles on
to wrestle with rebuilding
from a better plan
in view of what is sure to come

God of compassion,
I know that I need conversion
and look about for another John
to motivate me
stir up my energy for change
I know what I must do
but falter at the water's edge
give me the push, O God,
that will bring me to my senses
Amen

Terms of the Covenant

I bore you up on eagle wings and brought you here to myself.
Therefore, if you hearken to my voice and keep my covenant, you shall
be my special possession, dearer to me than all other people, though
all the earth is mine.

Exodus 19:4–5

look here's the deal:
I will be your God
and you will be my people
I agree to cherish and protect you
see you safely home
fill your land with milk and honey
and you will be dear to me
and holy
bearing a family likeness as any children do
let me spell it out for you:
stay close by me
worshiping no other
and you will learn my ways
become gracious of heart
and soft of speech
strengthening your elders
respecting your brother's life
your sister's goods
keeping your words honest
your desires pure
your marriages faithful
and we will keep the Sabbath, you and I
so we do not become strangers
forgetful of our agreement

in a nutshell:
you will become the holy people of a holy God
and I the answer to your prayers
harbor of your hopes
rock you build upon
and you will know the savior when he comes

Spirit of God
your law is just
and life giving

its taste is sweeter than honey
grant me the grace to live by its discipline
confident of its stability
respectful of its integrity
open its meaning to me
when I enter new lands
respond to new demands
teach me and my students to walk in its light
not slavishly
but as your dearest children
Amen

Prodigal Love

*While he was still a long way off, his father caught sight of him, and
was filled with compassion.*

Luke 15:20

one child left to claim a life, a name, a self
but came back empty-handed
he received without deserving
signs of prodigal forgiveness
outrageous love
the other child stayed
servant safe
in his father's house
finally he spoke up
asked for signs of love he had not dared to trust
the father
foolish as only fathers can be
put it all on the line
"everything I have is yours"
two boys learned a single lesson
the first, that love alone gives life
the other, that he himself
and not his work
was treasure in his father's eyes

loving, prodigal God,
I suppose I am more often
the child who feels unappreciated
than the child who turns away
yet I see both children when I look
closely in my mental mirror
let this insight inform my teaching
let me give students
space to name themselves
tell of homes and hurts and hopes
let me notice the silent ones
and invite them to tell their story
let me show an understanding heart
to each of them
and smile often
Amen

Mary

Blessed are you among women, and blessed is the fruit of your womb.

Luke 1:42

Mary was a woman of singular grace
really just a girl
attentive to prayer
to the hopes of her people
ready to answer yes
when everything in heaven and on earth
depended on her
of course she was "troubled" by the news,
the invitation
to yield her human flesh
to the works of God
to make possible a new creation
a new beginning to the story of deliverance

we are still troubled by it
and we weren't even there
yet in a certain sense
we were all there
children of the faithful remnant
past, present, and yet to be born
waiting as she did
for the moment of revelation
of invitation
of grace, of yes

Hail Mary, full of grace
sent as a blessing to us all
teach us to pray honestly
as you did
teach us to ponder all these things
in order to add our own yes

Holy Mary, mother of God
first to know the promised Messiah, pray for us
first disciple, pray for us
first to bring Good News
across the rugged roads of Palestine, pray for us

Hail, Mother of the Church
closest icon of the Holy One, pray for us
friend in our saddest moments, pray for us
spiritual grandmother of our children
help us to tell your story
in a way that will draw them closer to God
divine source of unending love and mercy
Amen

Ordinary Time: Summer, Fall

All Saints

I had a vision of a great multitude, which no one could count, from every nation, race, people and tongue. They stood before the throne and before the Lamb, wearing white robes and holding palm branches in their hands.

Revelation 7:9

in our world
autumn leaves vibrant with color
spend their last days
forcing themselves on our attention
demanding that we stop and see
and join in their awesome praise of the Creator

just so the Church calls our attention
to a stunning array of saints
the most colorful among our people
martyrs, mystics, bishops, and bricklayers
married and single, pious and unruly
recovered sinners of every sort

(even, dare I say it,
parish catechists make the list)
like dancing leaves
they force us to marvel at the ways of nature
transformed by grace
they are a cloud of witnesses
a communion of the sanctified
each with a story to tell
come, they say, join the great procession
come with us to the throne
as you were born to do
with juggler's bells and ribbons in your hair

Loving God
source of delight
show me your grace in the lives of the saints
that I may learn the diversity of possibilities
in Christian life
that I may appreciate the extraordinary holiness
of ordinary people
and the ordinary holiness
of the extraordinary people around me
help me to paint for my students
a vision of our glorious family of faith
who invite us into their parade
who watch our backs in dangerous times
who show us how Christianity is lived
joyfully
with flair
Amen

Ordinary Time: Summer, Fall

All Souls

I am the resurrection and the life; whoever believes in me, even if he dies, will live, and everyone who lives and believes in me will never die.

John 11:25–26

we do not want to die
we do not want the people we love to die
yet each day we move closer
to the moment of truth
the time of departure
the time when time ends
and ready or not
we or they
enter the final mystery
the Church strengthens and comforts us
helps us to gather our thoughts
renew our hope
you died at baptism, she says
and are already living in Christ
this physical death is a mirage
life changes but is not taken away
we make up a single communion of saints
joined to God through Christ
who willingly went through death for us
and shares his risen life with us
even now
therefore in peace
let us continue on

loving God
I commend to your sustaining mercy
each of my relatives and friends
who have died . . .

[name them, remember them]

let them know the full joy
of your presence
the full peace of your kingdom
help me to forgive their faults and failures
as you have forgiven them
let them watch over all the members of the family
who still struggle toward you in faith
reminding us of your unfailing mercy
your unchanging kindness
Amen

Our Lord Jesus Christ, King of the Universe

The chief priests of the Jews said to Pilate, "Do not write 'The King of the Jews,' but that he said, 'I am the King of the Jews.' " Pilate answered, "What I have written, I have written."

John 19:21–22

each knew the role of religion in politics
rulers need to be seen
offering incense to the proper gods
and claiming divine authorization
for the exercise of power in the public square
each knew the role of politics in religion
the claim of sole access to the divine ear
signs of precedence to awe the pious
formation of a band of cronies
to help build support among the gullible

each knew the stakes
the one who came from Rome
to keep the people quiet
with a puppet king and free access to the temple
and the other who came from Nazareth
with a message of God's love
and power to teach and heal in God's name
who had been avoiding the title of king
and the ambition it generated among his followers

so their conversation
left much unsaid
but understood between them
Are you the king of the Jews?
My kingdom does not belong to this world.

and in the end
whether through irony or mockery
the death sentence read:
Jesus the Nazorean
King of the Jews

Jesus
savior king
you know the strength of human ambition
to corrupt even the most important relationships
help my students
decipher in the biblical account of your life
as well as in the Church
authentic leadership
that builds on love and mutual support
that seeks to serve
and to set free
Amen

Praying with
Students and Colleagues

Ordinary Times

Dedication of the Year

Leader: Speak, Lord; your servants are listening.

All: Speak, Lord; your servants are listening.

Leader: Incarnate Word,
divine Mystery spoken in the heart of God
yet alive among us,
speak to us this year
as we gather in your name
and open ourselves to your word.

Speak to us through the sacred stories
of our people,
though the questions we ponder,
the encouragement we give one another.
Speak to us through our study
and our efforts to teach well.

Speak to us through the wisdom and trust
of students as they share experiences
of your goodness and care.
Awaken our gratitude for this opportunity
to hear you in each other's voices.

Reveal yourself to those of us
who are not attentive
to the immediacy of your presence,
or are unable to put into our own words
the wonder of your creation,
the dignity of your call,
the joy of your redeeming grace.

Word of God,
speak to us in this sacred conversation.
Speak, Lord; your servants are listening.

All: Speak, Lord; your servants are listening.
Amen.

Ordinary Times

Prayer before a Meeting

God of endless kindness,
help us to be of one mind
as we address the tasks of this gathering.
Bless us with wisdom and insight
that our deliberations may be crisp and fruitful.
Bless us with generosity and good judgment
that we may strengthen our work as catechists
and parents.

Bless us with joy in our companionship
and grace in our conversation
that our gathering may reflect
the true nature of your Church.

Bless us with love, dedication, and creativity
in the ministry of your word.

We ask this through your Son, Jesus Christ,
who lives and reigns with you
and with the Holy Spirit,
one God
for ever and ever.
Amen.

Ordinary Times

Prayer before Study or Preparation of Lessons

[Change the pronouns if you are praying with a group.]

Come, Holy Spirit;
be my witness and inspiration this day
that my study may be fruitful
and my teaching effective.

Spirit of Truth,
guide my reflections
that I may grasp in some measure
the coherence of your plan,
the graciousness of your revelation,
and the steady purpose of your saving love.

Spirit of Unity,
inspire my teaching
that I may awaken the passion of my students
to seek the truth,
to rely on your presence,
and to delight in the world you open up before them.

Spirit of Love,
grant me an understanding heart
that I may be a good and faithful teacher—
wise, well prepared,
confident in your guidance
and joyful in my calling.

I ask this in Jesus' name.
Amen.

Blessing and Dismissal of Students I

God, you are faithful in all things
and loving toward all you have created.
Look kindly on [*these students, N. and N.*].
Protect them from harm.
Strengthen them in spirit and body.
Bless them with . . .

[Make your blessing authentic and specific: e.g. curiosity, energy,
whole-heartedness, a sense of humor.]

and give them peace.

We ask this through Christ our Savior.
Amen.

Ordinary Times

Blessing and Dismissal of Students II

Kind and loving God,
source of all unity,
bless us on our way
that we may carry your love
in our hearts, our hands, and our voices
to those who are waiting
to welcome us home.

Let us bring joy to them,
protect and forgive them,
and share in their work and their worries.

Teach all in our family to value what is good,
to avoid what is dangerous,
to discover what is wonderful,
to respect what is sorrowful,
to strengthen one another,
and to remember always that Christ
is a guest at our table.
Amen.

Ordinary Times

Prayer for Students

Peter said, "I have neither silver nor gold, but what I do have I give you: in the name of Jesus Christ the Nazorean, [rise and] walk."

Acts 3:6

the faces of my students
like their hearts
are open, vulnerable, trusting
waiting for the clarity I bring
waiting for the good news
that Christ and the Church
have entrusted to me
waiting for my encouragement
to rise and walk
through their own strength and grace

*I am a fragile reed, O God
on which to pin your hopes
neither scholar nor saint
yet I am passionate
that they hear the full story of your love
from one who walks with you in faith*

*let my teaching be as living water
nourishing the seeds of faith
that you have planted
let your abundant grace
make up for my lack of skill
let your Holy Spirit
inspire our study, our conversations
and our prayer
Amen*

Ordinary Times

Prayer at a Time of Death in the Community

Leader: God of mercy,
we are filled with sorrow at the death of *N.*,
our colleague/relative/friend.
We celebrate her/his life and goodness,
and remember her/his many gifts.

[Mention something particular and/or invite comments by those present.]

Welcome her/him
into the great company of saints
who have known and loved you
and who now share in your glory.

God of compassion,
comfort all those who will miss the blessing
of her/his presence and love.
Grant that we may always remember her/him
with fondness and gratitude.

We ask this in the name of your Son,
Jesus Christ,
in whose risen life we are all united.

All: Amen.

Leader: Eternal rest grant unto her/him, O Lord.

All: And let perpetual light shine upon her/him.

Leader: May she/he rest in peace.

All: Amen.

Leader: May her/his soul
and the souls of all the faithful departed,
through the mercy of God,
rest in peace.

All: Amen.

Seasonal Blessings

Advent: Blessing of the Wreath

[The wreath can be incensed or sprinkled with holy water.]

Jesus Christ is the light of the world,
a light no darkness can overpower.

Gracious God, bless ✛ this wreath
as a sign of your covenant with us.
Bless all who gather around it
during this holy season of Advent
to remember the coming of your Son, Jesus Christ,
and to call on him to come again into our lives
this year
when all is in darkness,
so that we can be led by his light
and fed by his teaching
until the final day,
when he comes in glory
to lead us home.

Jesus Christ is the light of the world,
a light no darkness can overpower.

Seasonal Blessings

Christmas: Blessing of the Stable

God's holy day has dawned for us at last;
come, all you peoples, and adore the Lord.

Liturgy of the Hours for Epiphany

the couple reaches Bethlehem at last
but all the city can offer weary travelers
is safe shelter in a stable
a private place of birth
and unimaginable joy
a place to rest and pray and rejoice
before the child becomes
a public person
a name for the census
a new presence
that will realign the world

there are just a few at first
who defy the darkness and come
shepherds summoned by angels' song
and foreign scholars with well-chosen gifts
but multitudes soon will follow

let us linger at the stable
and ponder the meaning of all these things
with Mary, treasuring them in our hearts

Gracious God, bless + this sacred image.
Let it be a sign to us of the glad tidings
we too treasure in our hearts.
With the shepherds,
we glorify you for all we have heard and seen.
With the angels we sing of our joy.
Amen.

[End with carols.]

Seasonal Blessings

Epiphany: Blessing for the Gathering Space (or Home)

Around the time of Epiphany, gather at the entry door of the gathering space (or home). Use a piece of chalk to write an inscription over the door. The inscription includes initials for the names traditionally associated with the magi—Caspar, Melchior, and Balthasar. The letters also stand for *Christus mansionem benedicat* ("May Christ bless this house"). Place the first two digits of the year's date in front of the initials and the last two digits at the end. The marking for 2015 would be 20 + C + M + B + 15.

After marking the doorway, those who have assembled pray:

Leader: Peace be with this house
and with all who dwell in it.

All: Blessed be God for ever.

Leader: May all who visit us this year
find Christ
among those studying (dwelling) here.
And may we serve in every guest
the Christ by whom we all are blest.

All: Blessed be God for ever.

Amen.

Seasonal Blessings

Lent: Thanksgiving for Ashes

Merciful God,
in the dead of winter
as Lent begins,
I welcome the ashes
and the reminder that soon enough
I will bid this world good-bye.
My plans and projects,
my carefully built towers,
I myself
will fall to dust.
Yet I believe that spring will come,
that I will rise,
that all will be well
as you have promised.
Amen.

Lent: Prayer for Penitents

God of boundless mercy,
bless my students and their families
who seek your forgiveness
in the sacrament of reconciliation.
Grant them a realistic sense of their failures
but also of their goodness.
Grant them a wise confessor,
a comforting awareness of your presence,
and your delight in their love for you.
Help them to sort though
the rules, teachings, admonitions,
exhortations, and guidance they have been receiving
so they can focus on the disposition of their hearts:
determination to become
a more faithful follower of Jesus,
and the desire to make the world a safer,
more beautiful, loving place.
Send them back to us unburdened,
joyful,
and at peace.
Amen.

Seasonal Blessings

Lent: Preparation for Holy Week

The last class before Palm Sunday and Holy Week is usually spent in explaining the ceremonies of the most sacred days of the Christian calendar. Bring a few unblessed palms to show, along with the parish schedule of Holy Week services. Share the prayer below with the class.

Hosanna to the Son of David;
*   blessed is he who comes in the name of the Lord;*
hosanna in the highest.

Matthew 21:9

on Sunday we move with Jesus toward Jerusalem
take up green and supple branches
to cheer and sustain the One who sustains us
we know what is to come
the price he'll pay for bringing us this far
the cost of love

let these fragile palms
be woven into crosses
tucked behind pictures
honored in our family shrines
reminding us through the year
of the price he paid
reminding us of suffering and death
but even more
of life hard-won and worth the price
proclaiming anew the ancient gospel:
he goes ahead of us
on the path we all must walk
from joy and life
through death
and then to life again.

Loving God,
the Church is entering the most solemn days
in our year of remembrance and renewal.

Send your grace
that we may join the parish community
in experiencing the richness of
Holy Thursday, Good Friday, and Easter.
Grant us the gift of prayer
and teach us to be truly grateful
for the knowledge that our Savior lives.
Amen.

Easter: Prayer for the Newly Initiated

we watched through the night
as we were taught
lighted a new candle
blessed new water for the font
told stories around our little fire
remembering creation and covenant
love and rescue
sang Gloria and Alleluia
with full voice and trumpet
and they stood up and proclaimed their faith
the small band dressed in white
ready to join us on the journey
they rose from the water
washed in the blood of the Lamb
were anointed by the Spirit
embraced by the assembly
and at last came to the table
to be nourished and made whole
in the breaking of bread
in the blessing of peace

Risen Christ,
I am moved by their coming,
by their dignity and their faith,
and am happy to share in their joy.
Grant them the grace of perseverance
and make us, their catechists,
remain alert to their questions
when they see the flaws in our community,
when their energy begins to flag,
when the honeymoon is over
and they are faced with the difficulties
of committed love.
Then give me words to encourage them.
Help me to reach out in companionship.
Gracious God,
renew the baptismal freshness in us all.
Amen. Alleluia.

Seasonal Blessings

Easter Season: Blessing of First Communicants

Dear friends,
we rejoice
and celebrate with you
in the name of the whole Church
as you receive for the first time
the most sacred Body and Blood of Jesus.

We thank God for the grace given to you,
and for the witness you are giving to this community
through your eagerness to draw closer to Jesus,
through your love for God, the Father of Jesus,
through your desire to live in the peace
given by the Holy Spirit,
and through all of the prayer,
the study, and the preparation
that have brought you to this happy day,
when you will experience
with the whole Church
the full celebration of the Eucharist.

May God bless + you, and may Christ
dwell in your hearts through faith;
that you, rooted and grounded in love,
may have strength to comprehend with all the holy ones
what is the breadth and length and height and depth,
and to know the love of Christ that surpasses knowledge,
so that you may be filled with all the fullness of God.

Ephesians 3:17–19

Seasonal Blessings

Pentecost: Blessing of the Newly Confirmed

The Spirit of the Lord is upon me,
because he has anointed me
to bring glad tidings to the poor.

Luke 4:18

Spirit of God, Holy Wisdom,
we thank you for *N. [or "these students"]*
who has/have deepened *[or "who will deepen"]*
her/his/their commitment to you and to the Church
through the sacrament of confirmation.

Bless **+** and strengthen them.
Increase their reverence for the ways of the Church
their knowledge of the ways of the world,
their understanding of the dignity of all people.
Give them wisdom to seek the heart of things,
right judgment in all their decisions,
courage to live by what they believe.
Let them always experience
awe and wonder at the grace
and the gift of life itself.

Come, Holy Spirit,
fill the hearts of your faithful
and kindle in them the fire of your love.

Send forth your Spirit and they shall be created,
and you will renew the face of the earth.

Lord, by the light of the Holy Spirit
you have taught the hearts of your faithful.
In the same Spirit
help us to relish what is right
and always rejoice in your consolation.
Amen.

Praying for the World

For the Nation

Unless the LORD build the house,
*   they labor in vain who build.*
Unless the LORD guard the city
*   in vain does the guard keep watch.*

Psalm 127:1

At this time of national celebration and remembrance,
let us pray:

Loving God,
grant that all in our nation may flourish here
and live in peace.
Bless those who rejoice in the gift of life.
Bless those who promote justice, liberty, equality,
and human dignity.
Bless those who risk everything
for the safety of others.

God of unity,
help us to strengthen the communities
in which we live.
Bless those who give themselves to public service.
Bless those who welcome the immigrant,
provide for the vulnerable,
comfort the sorrowful, and care for the children.

God of wisdom and peace,
grant us the courage to move beyond
narrow self-interest.
Bless those who speak truth to power.
Bless those who reject violence and work for peace
in the neighborhood, the nation, and the world.

Bless those who through generous gifts
of their resources
contribute to the common good.

Creator God,
teach us to protect the bountiful land
entrusted to our care.
Bless those who work to restore the integrity
of the earth.
Bless those who celebrate its fragile beauty
in poetry and song.
Bless those who study the earth and its universe.

God of our ancestors,
teach us to hold our citizenship as a sacred trust,
so that our lives and our nation
will bring honor to you
and blessings to the human family.

We commend our citizens,
and indeed our nation itself,
to your grace and your mercy
as we celebrate . . .

[name the day or season of celebration].

Amen.

At a Time of Natural Disaster or Other Crisis

In my misfortune I called,
the LORD heard and saved me from all distress.

Psalm 34:7

God of mercy,
we gather in prayer for our brothers and sisters of . . .

[name the place, the situation].

As you were with Jesus in the Garden of Gethsemane,
be with them in their suffering.
Strengthen and console them now
and be their light and their strength
in the dark days to come.

Receive those who have died,
comfort those who are grieving,
rescue those who are trapped.
Heal the injured,
protect the rescue teams,
inspire all who can to send aid.

Strengthen all the victims;
calm their fears
and bring them peace.

Lord God,
life is a mystery
and suffering a certainty.
Let your light shine
in the hearts of all
who have experienced this disaster,
and in the hearts of all who live in hope
and in solidarity with them.
Amen.

For World Peace

They shall beat their swords into plowshares
and their spears into pruning hooks;
one nation shall not raise the sword against another,
nor shall they train for war again.

Isaiah 2:4bc

God of all nations,
protector of all peoples,
we come to you in a time of wars and revolutions
to pray for peace.
We pray especially for . . .

[mention the nations, cities, neighborhoods for whom you pray].

For these people and all who are at war today,
we ask the grace of strength, courage, comfort,
and wisdom.

We pray also for our own people.
Make us capable of living in peace
by transforming our customary
ways of thinking and acting.

Purify our relationships in the community of nations,
that the wealthy may not exploit the weak
or sponsor corruption.

Purify our memories,
that we do not nurture thoughts of hatred
and revenge
or seek retribution for past injuries.

Purify our ambitions,
that we may not seek
what cannot be had without damage to our neighbor
or to the environment.

Purify our sense of privilege and entitlement
to resources that are given for the benefit of all.

God of mercy,
inspire us to work for peace,
to train for peace,
to nurture the sparks of peace
wherever they are found.
Show us how to lead our students and families
in the ways of peace,
placing our trust and hope in you
and not in violence.

We ask this through
Jesus Christ, your Son.
Amen.

For Christian Unity

I have other sheep that do not belong to this fold. These also I must lead, and they will hear my voice, and there will be one flock, one shepherd.

John 10:16

shepherd of a single flock
so Jesus styles himself
yet stop for a minute
and see how scattered are his people
divided in belief, in prayer, in language,
in visions of the Christian goal

can Jesus be so splintered
his body so diffuse and contradictory
without losing the very Spirit
that is the living soul of his Church

how lightly we hold this imperative for unity
how accepting of the separated status quo
how far we have come from the common life
established at great cost by Christians of the
apostolic age

what would it take to reclaim our passion
to seek out other Christians
speak with clarity regarding faith
listen with an open mind to stories of
Christian life in other cultures, other languages
open our hearts to Christians facing other dangers
bearing other crosses

what would it take to dialogue with difference,
to search as one for Christian authenticity
work together for a just society
what would it take to set us on fire
once again

Come, Shepherd of the Church;
renew in us the vision
and the hope of true unity
among your people.

You have declared our unity as fact,
not mere ideal;
teach us to recognize and cultivate it.
Teach us again a common language,
that our dialogue may be fruitful,
our stories instructive,
our practices an open book.
Show us how "to live
in a manner worthy of the call
[we] have received,
with all humility and gentleness,
with patience,
bearing with one another through love,
striving to preserve the unity of the spirit
through the bond of peace" (Ephesians 4:1–4).
Amen.

For the Jewish People

Blessed are you,
Lord our God,
Ruler of the universe,
for you have loved and chosen a people,
leading them through deserts of hatred
and raging seas of prejudice,
remaining with them
in lands of exile and struggle.

Grant to our Jewish brothers and sisters
security in their homes throughout the world
and the freedom to worship
in dignity and peace.

Let their fidelity to you in the midst of suffering
and their joy in your service
be a witness to the covenant of love
you have made with them.

[If the occasion is a feast day or celebration, add the following:]

We commend them to your grace and your mercy
as they celebrate *[name the holy day or season]*.

Amen.

For the Muslim People

God most merciful, most compassionate,
open our hearts to our Muslim neighbors.
Increase our understanding of all who embrace Islam
and share our belief in you,
the One God.

Let their fidelity to the Holy Qur'an
and devotion to traditions
of prayer, fasting, charity, and pilgrimage
witness to the grace of their calling.

Grant our Muslim brothers and sisters
security in their homes throughout the world
and the freedom to worship
in dignity and peace.

Inspire Christians and Muslims alike
to treat one another
with justice and respect,
so that all may finally be united
in that peace that has its source in you,
the One God.

[If the occasion is a feast day or celebration, add the following:]

We commend them to your grace and your mercy
as they celebrate *[name the holy day or season]*.

Amen.

For Seekers

Protect, O God,
all those who honestly seek your face
amid the confusion of a busy life
in a fragmented world.

Some have never known the embrace
of a believing community.
Some reject outright the customary path of religion
because of what it is
or seems to be,
because of what it entails
or fails to offer,
because of its complicity in violence and scandal
or its perceived complexity.

A thousand causes
with but one result:
they seek your face
and do not see it reflected
in the people and practices of religion.

Bless and keep them in safety,
God of mercy.
Place faithful communities,
honest prophets,
and loving teachers along their way,
and let them know your presence
in the quiet dedication of their hearts.
Amen.

Scripture Index

Elizabeth McMahon Jeep

Elizabeth Jeep is the Associate Director of the St. Catherine of Siena Center of Dominican University in River Forest, Illinois, where she teaches a Sophomore Seminar and courses for the university's School of Continuing Learning. She is a theologian specializing in religious education and holds a doctorate in religion and psychology from Chicago Theological Seminary, and a master's degree from The Catholic University of America. She is the founding author of *Children's Daily Prayer for the School Year*, as well as *Blessings and Prayers through the Year, Children's Daily Prayer for the Summer, Blessed be God*, and *The Welcome Table: Celebrating the Eucharist with Children*. Dr. Jeep serves on the Archdiocesan Catechist Certification Commission and is on the boards of the Children's Spirituality Conference and the Chicago Coalition for InterReligious Learning. She is a charter member of the dialogue sponsored by the Archdiocese of Chicago and the Council of Islamic Organizations of Greater Chicago.

Other Titles in the *Pray Today* Series

Ringing True: Prayers for Handbell Ringers
   by Linda Stahelin

Gathered to Serve: Prayers for Parish Leaders
   by Jerry Galipeau

Guided by Grace: Prayers for Worship Committees
   by Michael R. Prendergast

Be with Me, Lord: Prayers for the Sick
   by Rodney J. DeMartini

In Holy Harmony: Prayers for Parish Musicians
   by Alan J. Hommerding

Called to Be Your Song: Prayers for Cantors
   by Michael E. Novak

Servant of the Lord: Prayers for Deacons
   by Deacon Peter Hodsdon

Enlightened by Faith: Prayers for the RCIA Journey
   by Anita Ahuja

*Psalms from the Heart: Prayers for the Times
   and Seasons of Faith* by Marion van der Loo